Original title:
Breezes in the Birches

Copyright © 2025 Creative Arts Management OÜ
All rights reserved.

Author: Sebastian Whitmore
ISBN HARDBACK: 978-1-80567-312-5
ISBN PAPERBACK: 978-1-80567-611-9

Whispers Through the Willows

The willows gossip, oh so slight,
With secrets shared in morning light.
A squirrel drifts by, a nut in tow,
He's fashionably late, but steals the show.

The dandelions chuckle, heads held high,
While daisies declare, 'Oh, me? Just shy!'
The grasshoppers leap, with shoes too tight,
They trip on dew and dance in flight.

Caress of the Dancing Leaves

The leaves perform their swaying dance,
Each twirl a silly, leafy prance.
A butterfly joins, with a wink so sly,
Saying, 'Watch my moves,' as it flits by.

A gust of wind gives them a shove,
'Careful now,' they shout, 'not so tough, love!'
Yet tumble they do, in a leafy heap,
A nature's comedy, a laugh to keep.

Murmurs Beneath the Canopy

Underneath the leafy shield,
Crickets chirp their fate revealed.
A raccoon sneaks, so sly and slick,
With shiny eyes and a playful trick.

The shadows giggle, as they play,
A game of tag, come join the fray!
But oh, a branch, poor raccoon prance,
Now worries more of his mischance.

Soft Winds and Silver Leaves

Soft winds swirl, with a gentle tease,
They tickle the toes of crickets with ease.
Buttercups giggle, as they bend and sway,
'We're all in a rush, it's a fun-filled day!'

The river sings, a silly tune,
While ducks play catch with a fallen moon.
A raccoon's laugh echoes near the stream,
In this wild patch, all is a dream.

Swaying Silhouettes Against the Light

Branches dance with quirky grace,
Leaves prance round in a dizzy chase.
A squirrel trips, falls with flair,
"Sorry folks!" it shouts with a messy hair.

Shadows stretch in the sunlight's gleam,
They twist and turn like a wild dream.
Caught in laughter, skies so blue,
Dance on, trees, we're laughing too!

Flourish of Nature's Breathe

Winds whisper jokes, they tease the bark,
Leafy laughter leaves its mark.
A chipmunk tells a pun so bad,
The owls just roll their eyes and add.

The branches wiggle, ruffled glee,
A tree trunk's boggy chortle, see?
With every rustle, fun takes flight,
In this leafy, lively, silly sight.

Soothing Touch of Dappled Light

Sunbeams tickle the forest floor,
Each shimmer plays like a game of lore.
A tiny bug dons a cape of flight,
Strikes a pose in the sudden light.

Fluttering leaves spread laughter's song,
A bumblebee hums right along.
Nature's stage, full of delight,
A comical scene, oh what a sight!

The Grace of Luminous Leaves

Leaves gossip softly as they sway,
Chatting about the cute chipmunk's play.
The twigs giggle, not a single care,
As acorns drop, they bounce in the air.

A dance-off starts with a gusty cheer,
Swirling the laughter of every deer.
In this bright folly, joy takes flight,
Nature's humor bathed in light.

Nurtured by the Calm

In a forest full of whispers,
A squirrel steals the show,
With acorns piled like treasure,
He smiles with a cheeky glow.

The trees all shake in laughter,
As he trips over his stash,
His friends roll on the ground,
While their giggles make a splash.

The sun peeks through the branches,
Like a prankster in disguise,
Chasing shadows in a dance,
With a wink in its warm eyes.

Dance, dance, oh wobbling leaves,
In a game of peek-a-boo,
No worries for tomorrow,
Just the fun of today's view.

Flickering Moments Between Boughs

Two robins in a ruckus,
Playing tag up in the sky,
One slips on a tiny twig,
And they both go tumbling by.

The branches jiggle in delight,
As if they're laughing too,
With the rustling of the leaves,
And the sun shining through.

A game of hide and seek ensues,
With tiny creatures on the run,
Whiskers twitching, tails flicking,
Underneath the golden sun.

Oh the joy that nature brings,
In every playful prank,
For under arches of the trees,
The world is free to thank.

Celestial Air Dancing Amongst Green

A breeze that tickles petals,
Whispers jokes to birds above,
"Why did the tree go to school?"
"To get a little more trunk love!"

The daisies laugh in patches,
Spinning tales beneath the sky,
As clouds roll in, all fluffy,
Like marshmallows floating by.

The grass sways in the rhythm,
Of a funky, silly tune,
While ladybugs are jiving,
In a dance beneath the moon.

Nature's humor knows no bounds,
With each giggle in the air,
In this green and growing world,
Every creature finds a share.

Enchanted Voices of the Woods

A toad croaks a melody,
While crickets chime along,
Together they form a symphony,
In a quirky, woodland song.

The owls are wise and watchful,
But they wink without a care,
"For in the night we revel,
And dance without a spare!"

The moon giggles in the shadows,
As fireflies flash their lights,
Setting off a sparkling fireworks,
In these whimsical nights.

Oh, the laughter in the green,
Echoes through the trees so tall,
In this enchanted haven,
Nature's joy unites us all.

Harmony in the Rustle and Whisper

In the woods all critters play,
Frogs wear socks and dance all day.
Squirrels giggle, birds take flight,
Chasing sticks, what a sight!

Leaves are clapping, trees can't wait,
Bunnies line-dance, it's first-rate.
A raccoon with a ukulele strums,
While a bear hums to the drums.

Sunlight flickers through the trees,
Bees wear hats to catch the breeze.
A hedgehog sings, it's quite a show,
While ants form lines, with hats in tow.

Folks may say this forest's tame,
But here, they play a silly game.
As shadows dance and laughter swirls,
Nature's joy unfurls and twirls!

Shadows Merging in the Glade

In the glade where shadows meet,
Toads are tap-dancing on tiny feet.
Hares in top hats, quite the scene,
Mice on scooters, they reign supreme!

Fungi giggle, moss joins in,
While dragonflies play hide and spin.
With twinkling eyes, they share a cheer,
Comedic flair from every sphere.

A snail slips by wearing a grin,
Challenging a worm, let the race begin!
But oh, what fun, they all agree,
Finish line's under that big oak tree.

Whispers float through the sunny air,
As all participate, but do they care?
With echoes of laughter, they leave a trail,
In this glade, joy prevails!

The Calm Before Today's Adventure

Before the fun, they gather round,
A gang of critters, no one's profound.
Chirpy birds plan a great big scheme,
While a fox insists it's all a dream.

Tumbles and fumbles, what a mess,
A hedgehog's wardrobe, we must confess!
With mismatched socks and a jaunty hat,
Dressing up is where it's at!

They clap their paws and flap their wings,
Counting down to whatever spring brings.
With eager hearts and twinkling eyes,
Ready to take off to the skies!

But first, they snack on nuts and seeds,
Rabbits nibble on tasty weeds.
Then it's go time, the countdown's begun,
In the moments before the fun!

Airborne Murmurs in Autumn's Glow

In autumn's glow, the leaves do sway,
While owls crack jokes, what a display!
Squirrels are plotting, full of glee,
A treasure hunt for acorns, you see?

With every gust, the laughter grows,
As chipmunks share their dancing woes.
They wobble and bob, make quite the scene,
Twirling 'round like a well-dressed bean.

Pinecones tumble, causing a ruckus,
While a beaver, oh my, yells, "That's just us!"
With hats of leaves, they prance and glide,
Comedic antics, they cannot hide.

So when the sun sets, and shadows play,
In that crisp air, they chase away gray.
For in this fun, beneath the trees,
Are hearts so light, on autumn's breeze!

The Language of Woodland Whispers

In the woods where squirrels scamper,
Leaves chat softly, whispers pamper.
A branch snaps loud, a bird takes flight,
Laughter echoes in morning light.

The raccoons play a game of tags,
Frogs take turns, they jump like jags.
A butterfly winks with a twist,
Nature's humor can't be missed.

The trees gossip, a rustling spree,
As chipmunks dance like they're on TV.
A breeze tickles, they all comply,
Nature's giggles drift through the sky.

With every gust, a chuckle sounds,
As leaves swirl fast, the fun abounds.
In this realm of playful sound,
The woods wear joy, joy unbound.

Playful Breezes and Shimmering Shades

In the shade where shadows play,
The sunbeams laugh, it's quite a ballet.
Frogs croak jokes upon the lily,
Dancing fireflies sing, oh so silly.

A gust whooshes by with flair,
Rustling whispers fill the air.
A chipmunk jokes, a squirrel nods,
Together they share their little odds.

With every turn, the leaves all swirl,
A windy waltz causing a twirl.
Nature's merry, funny parade,
In this vibrant glade, joy is made.

When the moon peeks, it joins the fun,
Starry eyes watch, the laughter runs.
In shadows deep, the night grows bold,
Whispers of cheer, forever told.

Threads of Air Through the Leaves

In the canopy, where secrets dwell,
Winds weave stories, a playful spell.
Leaves shake hands, making a pact,
To tease the breeze, that's a fact.

A dandelion seeds take flight,
Floating off like little kites.
A giggle here, a flutter there,
The forest sings with glee to spare.

Rabbits stomp in a silly race,
While bees buzz by in their haste.
A breeze tickles, they jump and twine,
Laughter bubbles from root to vine.

Each rustle brings a joke or two,
In nature's realm, fun is the glue.
With threads of air, the trees all sway,
In this merry dance, we laugh and play.

A Gentle Hum of Nature

The hum of woods, a gentle tease,
Leaves sashay dancing with the breeze.
The brook giggles, splashes around,
Rustling laughter is all around.

A rabbit hops with great delight,
While fireflies twinkle through the night.
Crickets chirp their funny tune,
Under the smile of a glowing moon.

With each rustle, there's a wink,
A dancing leaf, a playful slink.
Nature chuckles in warm embrace,
Every green corner holds a face.

As night descends, the tales unfold,
In whispers soft, both brave and bold.
From branches high to roots below,
Nature's humor puts on a show.

Secrets of the Silver Trunks

The trees tell tales, oh such delight,
Of squirrels that dance, in mid-flight.
A chipmunk with secrets up its sleeve,
Winks at the world, who would believe?

In shadows, they plot, with acorn spies,
Laughing so hard, they can barely rise.
One tree whispers to another old sage,
"Did you hear? The crow has gone on stage!"

They gossip of winds that fluffed their leaves,
And how the old owl slyly deceives.
"Did you see that robin with a flair?"
"Wearing a hat? Now that's quite rare!"

Under the moon, with a flicker and sway,
They chuckle at raccoons who play all day.
Secrets are shared, just rustles and fun,
In the realm of the trees, all join as one.

Murmurs of the Woodland

In the grove, a world unfolds,
With whispers at dawn, and stories retold.
The ferns hold giggles, the daisies cheer,
While the rabbits debate who's funnier here.

Moss-covered rocks wear a comical frown,
As the deer strut by in their 'fashion' gown.
The laughter of leaves fills the air so grand,
A boisterous jest from the woodpecker band!

Spiders weave webs, oh what a sight,
A glittering joke in the morning light.
As ants march in line, with a thump and a shout,
"Who needs a map when we've got this route?"

Whispers of each creature, with giggles they share,
A comedy show happening everywhere.
In the heart of the green, where joy is a must,
The woodland chuckles, it's more than just rust!

Rustling Dreams Under the Sky

With every gust, a story sways,
The saplings giggle in childhood plays.
A leaf, a hat; does it fit just right?
Perched on a squirrel, what a silly sight!

Each tumbleweed dances without a care,
Mimicking rabbits in a hilarious pair.
The clouds above join in the raucous fun,
As they shape-shift into a sandwich bun!

The grasses whisper, "Shhh, hear that noise?"
It's a squirrel's gathering of all the toys.
They argue over the best game of tag,
"Oh, you're it!"—and flea like a ragged flag!

Under the vastness where giggles collide,
Nature embraces this playful slide.
Rustling dreams float under moonlight's beam,
In the laughter of night, all creatures scheme.

Serenity Among the Saplings

In a cozy lane where the laughter flows,
Saplings giggle as the sunlight glows.
With each gentle sway, a ticklish tease,
"The ant over there, is it counting trees?"

Their leaves converse with a fluttering cheer,
A melody of mischief, delighting the ear.
"Did you hear the birch? It's in on the jest!"
"Claims it can dance better than all the rest!"

Chirping birds drop humorous notes,
As the fawns frolic on wobbly floats.
"Let's form a conga! Come join the line!"
The whole forest joins in without a sign!

Under moonlit skies, amidst laughter and dreams,
Nature spins tales in whimsical themes.
Serenity reigns, yet there's mischief anew,
Among the young trunks, the fun simply grew.

Wind-Kissed Leaves at Dusk

Leaves giggled in the twilight glow,
Dancing high, putting on a show.
A squirrel spun with a clumsy flair,
While branches swayed without a care.

Twisting tales in the golden light,
Whispering secrets, oh what a sight.
The wind joined in, a jester's laugh,
As shadows played on the forest's path.

Barking bugs hummed their silly tunes,
While owls crooned to the lazy moons.
The grass was tickled by a playful breeze,
As critters wobbled like knobby knees.

At dusk's embrace, all the world's a stage,
Each tree a performer, none are age.
With laughter echoing, they take their chance,
In this whimsically nature's dance.

The Breath of Forest Spirits

Whispers floated through the tangled wood,
Where giggling sprites played, as best they could.
A mossy goblin slipped on a stone,
In the playful antics, they'd never moan.

Critters chuckled at the strange parade,
As shadows pranced in the sun's cascade.
A deer took a leap that was rather bold,
But tripped on a twig, oh, how it trolled!

The breeze told jokes to the leaf-laden trees,
And branches swayed laughing like they were at ease.
With each breath, the forest felt alive,
As spirits frolicked, they seemed to thrive.

Their merry cacophony amused the night,
Felty whispers blinked in soft moonlight.
In harmony, they spun stories bright,
Of trickster tales and hilarious fright.

Lullabies of the Birchwood

Amidst the birches, snug and tight,
Whimsical whispers filled the night.
Crickets crooned with a comical beat,
As sleepy saplings shuffled their feet.

Each bark had tales too tall to share,
Of playful forest sprites beyond compare.
A squirrel sang, with a voice that crackled,
While the sleepy leaves softly cackled.

Night settled in, wrapped in quirky dreams,
While the branches swayed, all in teams.
Rustling leaves joined in soft refrains,
Like little puns carried on giddy veins.

In this wood, sleep's not so bland,
With laughter and mischief on every hand.
So snuggle tight, let the giggles flow,
In lullabies where the fun does grow.

Flickers of Light Through Green

Sunlight flickered through the leafy dome,
Making funny patterns that felt like home.
Each leaf seemed to wiggle and wink,
In the dance of shadows, they'd often think.

A wily fox with an exaggerated prance,
Joined in the rhythm of a leafy dance.
As sunbeams pirouetted, a bird took a dive,
All creatures chuckled, feeling alive.

The breeze tossed chortles through branches wide,
As shadows painted a quirky slide.
Mischief thrived where the sun rays shone,
In whimsical moments, all alone.

Nature's jester with a spark in its eye,
Chased giggles around as they floated by.
With flickers of joy in the glowing scene,
Life hummed a tune, so fresh and green.

Luminous Dreams Beneath the Canopy

The leaves dance with joy, oh what a sight,
Playing tag with the sun, in pure delight!
A squirrel dons shades, strutting with flair,
While a chipmunk makes music without a care.

Birds mistake a kite for a friend in the sky,
Chasing it wildly, oh me, oh my!
A gust gives a nudge, then off they soar,
In a wacky waltz, they go to explore.

The grass giggles softly, tickles the toes,
While a frog plays a tune nobody knows.
Bumblebees buzz in a jazzy parade,
As nature's own band starts to invade.

With laughter aloft, beneath leafy views,
Each rustle and whisper is full of clues.
In this canvas of green, whimsy unfurls,
Where the trees tell tales of their hidden pearls.

A Serenade of Shadows and Sun

In the glade, the shadows start to prance,
The sun plays peek-a-boo, daring to glance.
A rabbit giggles, its ears flop in glee,
As a butterfly winks, oh so cheekily.

A squirrel gets stuck, mid-leap in a tree,
As if the branches are bursting with glee.
The daisies all chuckle, waving their heads,
While owls make notes, writing comedy threads.

The songbirds compose a hilarious tune,
Songs of mishaps and dances 'neath the moon.
A thistle sings bass while a dandelion hums,
Creating a ruckus as laughter becomes.

In shadows that stretch on this bright, sunny day,
Nature's a jester, and here's what it says:
"Join the madcap, let worries subside,
For life's just a joke, with fun as our guide!"

Nature's Promise in the Whispering Wind

Gentle whispers swirl, secrets they share,
As ants march along, with a grand flair.
Each grass blade is tickled with soft, silly gales,
While a worm in a hat swoops low, then wails.

The clouds play toss with a wayward hat,
Landing on a sleepy cat who just sat.
While the flowers sway, shaking their heads,
In a garden of giggles where silliness spreads.

A dandelion dreams of becoming a star,
Wishing on wishes and wishing afar.
The trees shake with laughter, so loud and so bright,
In this merry orchestra from morning to night.

In this patch of joy, where chuckles blend in,
Life dances and twirls, spinning round with a grin.
For nature's a jester, in this world so alive,
Promising laughter, as all things will thrive.

Enigma of Twilight in the Grove

When twilight descends, and the stars start to peek,
The shadows grow longer, with secrets to speak.
A raccoon steals cookies, sneaky and spry,
While a lost firefly just wonders, "Why?"

As night falls near, crickets hold court,
Ribbiting quips as they laugh and cavort.
A frog in a beret tries out a new dance,
While the moon rolls its eyes at this curious chance.

The owls hoot in rhythm, a lyrical show,
More puzzled than wise, as wisdom we know.
And the trees hold their breath, waiting for pranks,
For twilight's a riddle, with giggles in banks!

So here in the grove, where the mysteries hum,
Life's playful spirit knows how to have fun.
In shadow and light, let laughter take flight,
For the enigma of night is a comedy bright!

Flickers of Sunlight through the Foliage

In the dance of sunlight's play,
Leaves twirl on a bright, silly day.
Critters giggle, shadows tease,
Nature's jokes blow in the breeze.

Squirrels hide acorns in odd spots,
While birds gossip with silly thoughts.
A lazy cat stretches with grace,
As a butterfly flutters, looking for space.

Branches sway with chuckles profound,
Whispers of laughter fill the ground.
Each flicker a secret spoken low,
In the canopy where silly things grow.

Sunbeams slip through, a glowing chain,
Laughter erupts like a soft champagne.
In this realm of light and whimsy,
Life's a joke, simple and Timsy.

Woven Vows of Leaf and Sky

Leaves promise the sky with a wink,
Binding their vows with a splash of pink.
Clouds float by, so fluffy and round,
With giggles that echo all over the ground.

Rooftops peek out, trying to hear,
Nature's romantic, giggling cheer.
Branches twist into odd shapes,
As squirrels plan their nutty capes.

Sunlight knits its golden thread,
While shadows murmur the tales they spread.
Up high, the ruckus and chime,
Reminds us all to laugh sometimes.

In this patch of leafy delight,
Vows are woven with joy so bright.
The dialogue of nature, so sly,
Turns beautiful, with each rustling sigh.

Secrets Shared with the Whispering Woods

In the secret nooks, whispers flow,
Branches gossip, friends in tow.
Beetles cheer with little grins,
As the curtain of twilight begins.

Mice in checkers play hide and seek,
With a dandelion, they share a peek.
Trees chuckle, their arms stretched wide,
In this game where laughter won't hide.

The giggle of a brook's soft song,
Crickets join in, they sing along.
Each rustle holds a tale anew,
A comedy played out beneath the blue.

The woods are alive with chuckles bright,
A symphony of mischief at night.
Secrets tumble like leaves that flow,
In this joyful wood where the fun does grow.

Tides of Air Among the Green Sentinels

Tides of air roll in waves of cheer,
Whispering whispers we're glad to hear.
Tall trunks sway as if to say,
"Join the prank, come out and play!"

Down below, grasshoppers leap,
In this terrain where joy runs deep.
Frogs croak jokes in croaky tones,
As laughter dances with little moans.

The wind carries tales from afar,
Each howl and whoosh, a lucky star.
Kites of color float up high,
While clouds drift past, oh my, oh my!

Underneath the leafy decree,
Nonsense blooms, wild and free.
In this world where the air is spry,
The green sentinels wink as they sigh.

Embrace of the Swaying Limbs

In a dance of leaves they sway,
Twisting gently, come what may.
A squirrel's waltz, a chipmunk's jig,
Nature's polka—oh so big!

A breeze that tickles soft and light,
Causing birds to take their flight.
They squawk and flap, a comical show,
As tree trunks giggle to and fro.

With every twist, a branch does tease,
Sending acorns down like peas.
A nutty mess, it bounces round,
As laughter echoes through the ground.

Nature's play placed on display,
Leaves clap hands, dance all day.
In silly circles, trees do spin,
Inviting all to join the din!

Twilight Hums Among the Trees

As twilight falls, the shadows grow,
The trees start humming, just for show.
A lullaby that breaks the night,
A frog hops in, joining the fright!

Crickets chirp their evening tune,
While owls whoop beneath the moon.
Springy spouts of laughter rise,
As wind rustles with silly sighs.

Branches sway with teasing grace,
A game of tag we can't replace.
A starlit party, pure delight,
As nature dances till first light.

Through leafy laughs and playful tricks,
The forest blends its funny mix.
In the evening's warm embrace,
Each rustle puts a grin on face!

Secrets in the Swaying Branches

What secrets hide where shadows creep,
In branches swaying, canopy deep?
A raccoon with a mask so bright,
Reveals its stash, oh what a sight!

Whispers float on a warm spring air,
Squirrels giggle without a care.
Branches play shy, but peek-a-boo,
As grinning owls say, "Who are you?"

A gentle rustle, a playful tease,
The wind teaches trees how to sneeze.
Leaves flutter down like confetti bright,
As secrets tumble in sheer delight.

With twigs that twist in mischief's game,
Each crackle sparks a jolly flame.
In this lively, leafy swirl,
Laughter dances, life in a whirl!

Choreography of the Forest's Breath

The forest shakes in rhythmic flow,
Dancing limbs put on a show.
A tug-of-war with gusts so sly,
Leaves tumble down, oh me, oh my!

A chorus of rustles fills the air,
Chirpy chirps, and whoops to share.
As branches twirl with graceful spins,
Even the roots laugh, giving grins!

Nature's ballet, grand and bright,
Waltzing 'neath the soft moonlight.
Pinecones roll like little logs,
A funny sight for passing frogs!

As twilight wraps the trees in cheer,
Their wiggly moves are loud and clear.
In this lively, jolly pageant true,
The forest breathes its dance anew!

Symphony of the Shivering Boughs

In the trees where branches sway,
Squirrels dance, they love to play.
Leaves applaud in cheeky glee,
Who's the top dancer? Wait and see!

Frogs jump in and raise a cheer,
While singing birds lend an ear.
Acorns drop, a clumsy show,
Nature's giggle, on we go!

Winds tickle roots beneath the ground,
With a whoosh, they make a sound.
Ticklish trunks shudder with fun,
In this woods, there's never one!

Join the laugh, let worries cease,
As the branches sway in peace.
Laughter echoes, bloom and grow,
In this grove, the joy's aglow!

Serenade in the Starlit Grove

Underneath the twinkling lights,
Owls hoot jokes on starry nights.
Moonbeams wink at all the trees,
Giggling softly with the breeze.

Bunnies hop in silly loops,
Chasing shadows, forming groups.
Fireflies flash their secret code,
In this dance, all thoughts erode.

Whispers float on gentle air,
As raccoons juggle without care.
A squirrel strums its tiny lute,
Making melodies, oh so cute!

Nature's ensemble never fades,
In this grove where laughter pervades.
Join the fun, let spirits soar,
In the night, we crave for more!

Laughter of the Rustling Foliage

Winds weave tales through leafy lanes,
As rustling laughter lifts our pains.
Chipmunks jest and make a fuss,
In a world that's all about us.

Twigs snap under playful paws,
Celebrating life with natural applause.
Nature's clowns, the birds take flight,
Mimicking sounds with pure delight.

Vines tickle branches, swirl around,
As if playing a merry sound.
Trees chuckle and sway in time,
It's nature's pixie, oh so prime!

Hidden critters all unite,
To share in this joyful plight.
So let's giggle, laugh, and cheer,
In this foliage, joy is near!

Gentle Currents in the Green

The leafy whispers have a tune,
Dancing lightly under the moon.
Every little critter's here,
To spread some joy and bring good cheer.

Grasshoppers hop in comic leaps,
As nature softly laughs and peeps.
With dragonflies that twirl and spin,
This playful game, we all jump in!

The tall grasses sway and tease,
With secrets shared in every breeze.
A picnic here, with ants and friends,
A laughter fest, that never ends!

In this park of lively glee,
Where every moment's free to be.
Join the chorus, shout with might,
For in this green, we hold the light!

The Language of Leaves in Motion

Leaves carry gossip from tree to tree,
Whispering secrets, how silly they be.
One says it's raining, the other just laughs,
While squirrels do acrobatics—oh, what gaffes!

Rustling with laughter, the branches all sway,
Chasing the clouds in a comical play.
A dance for the critters up high on the limbs,
In the theater of nature, oh, how it brims!

The wind tells a joke, and the leaves crack a grin,
Creating a chorus of joyful din.
They quiver and flutter, with glee they do prance,
In the fresh air of spring, they're all in a dance!

So listen closely to that leafy delight,
Their playful exchanges from morning to night.
Keep your ears open, don't let it be missed,
For the language of leaves is too fun to resist!

Caressing Shadows and Sunlight Dreams

When shadows are playful and sunlight is gold,
The trees wiggle softly, with tales to be told.
A game of tag starts, between sunbeams and shade,
As the branches all giggle—how easily swayed!

The trunks start to sway, in the glimmers of gleam,
And the leaves flurry up, like a wild, happy dream.
"Well, who gets the light?" one leaf shouts with pride,
While below, chubby ants just scuttle and hide.

The trees wear their shadows like hats on their heads,
Creating new patterns where no leaf shreds.
Dizzy from laughing in the dappled sun,
They play around freely, oh, what silly fun!

So come, take a seat, in the cool of the boughs,
Listen to whispers, and don't break your vows.
Share in the giggles of shadows that gleam,
In the sunlight's embrace, it's a whimsical dream!

Lullabies in the Gentle Glade

A gentle hum lulls a nap in the sun,
As leaves like lullabies, together they run.
They rustle and chatter, in tones soft and sweet,
While critters all cuddle, embracing their treat.

A sleepy-eyed owl gives a wide, silly yawn,
As the woodland bustles, just waking at dawn.
With mushrooms for pillows and ferns for their beds,
Tiny frogs croak softly, with dreams in their heads.

As fishtail clouds pass, they tickle the air,
And the leaves giggle softly, without a care.
"Snore softly," they whisper, "to rest you must go,"
In this lullaby forest, pure joy overflow.

So drift into dreams beneath branches so wise,
Where the moon bends down for a sweet, starry prize.
Beneath the gentle whispers, life dances and plays,
In the heart of the glade, where the magic stays!

A Tapestry of Leafy Sighs

Every sigh from the leaves, a story to tell,
Of the breezes that tickle, and all is quite swell.
They murmur and chuckle, in a patchwork of glee,
While sporting their hues, just so proud to be free!

A tapestry woven from laughter and light,
They sway with the stories of day and of night.
The golden sun winks, as the shadows all hide,
A chorus of chuckles, they simply can't bide.

"Hey, Leafy McTwist!" one leaf curtsies low,
"Don't dance too close to the trunk, or you'll slow!"
While dandelion fluff blows a kiss to a friend,
Creating a ruckus as they play till the end.

Look close, and you'll see, it's a whimsical sight,
Nature's own artistry, each leaf shining bright.
In this tapestry woven, there's nothing but cheer,
Where the sighs of the leaves bring the whole world near!

Heartbeats of the Forest

The trees do wiggle, it seems,
With their leafy dancing dreams.
Squirrels gossip, tails in a twist,
Nature's party, you can't resist.

Branches wave, a ticklish sight,
Whispering laughter, pure delight.
Mice in tuxedos roam about,
Wondering what life's all about.

A raccoon juggles fallen nuts,
While owls hoot in happy struts.
Twigs tap dance in playful pairs,
Even bushes join the flares.

As shadows stretch and sunlight fades,
The forest chuckles, full of jades.
With every heartbeat, laughter swells,
In this green kingdom where joy dwells.

Fluttering Memories in the Arbor

In a grove where giggles play,
Fluttering leaves jump in dismay.
A butterfly trips on its own wings,
Causing a ruckus, oh what it brings!

The rabbit bursts from leafy beds,
Wearing tiny hats upon its heads.
A deer prances, twirls with flair,
As crickets chirp a dance in air.

Leaves recall that funny day,
When a worm won in a high-stakes play.
Roots wiggle like they know the joke,
Every branch bends, and laughter's woke.

In this wood, absurdity reigns,
Where every creature, their humor gains.
With each rustle and whispered spree,
The memories flutter, wild and free.

Vibrations of Serenity

The trunks hum softly in the breeze,
Tickling the woods with gentle tease.
Frogs leap like they've got no care,
While birds serenade, their tunes so rare.

A family of ants in a line,
Takes a detour for some sweet vine.
Every rock hears the tales spun,
As echoing laughs unite as one.

Beneath their green, the soil's rich,
Worms throw parties without a hitch.
Ecosystems find their groove,
Each branch sways, as if to prove.

The quiet chuckles, small and bright,
Fill the forest with sheer delight.
In this realm where serenity sings,
Even the shadows join in on flings.

The Lull of Woodland Symphony

In the quiet of stacks of pine,
The air is thick with comic line.
Crickets clash their rhythm sticks,
While owls throw jokes like magic tricks.

Foxes prance on forgotten trails,
Chasing shadows and peppered tales.
A woodpecker with a nifty beat,
Drums out laughter, oh what a treat!

The stream giggles over smooth stones,
Making music with secret tones.
As sunlight filters through the leaves,
A symphony stirs, and joy believes.

All the critters join in a soft tune,
Under the watch of the glowing moon.
Together they weave a woodland spell,
In this lullaby, all is well.

Echoes of Gentle Winds

A wobbly branch waved at me,
Its dance was quite a sight to see.
A squirrel slipped, and oh, what luck!
It fell with style, just like a duck.

The leaves all whispered jokes so sly,
About the novice bird who tried to fly.
His first attempt ended in a thud,
Covered in twigs, he looked like mud.

The grass was laughing, rolling wide,
At the butterflies that couldn't hide.
One landed on a dog's big nose,
He sneezed, which struck a funny pose.

So when you stroll through woods so green,
Remember all the quirks unseen.
In nature's theater, take a seat,
And catch the acts that can't be beat.

Soft Sighs from the Grove

The branches gossip, twist, and bend,
As if they're sharing tales, my friend.
A bear with glasses reading leaves,
Found out that nature often deceives.

A rabbit hops, then trips on air,
The owl just stares with a blank glare.
He munches leaves, claims it's his treat,
While grasshoppers dance with tiny feet.

The sun peeks in, winks from afar,
And whispers to the evening star.
They chuckle softly, this cosmic pair,
As shadows play tag without a care.

Oh, these soft sighs from nature's crew,
Bring laughter fresh like morning dew.
So join their fun, lose track of time,
In this whimsical world, oh so sublime.

Twilight Musings of the Trees

At twilight, trees begin to chat,
Discussing who's the spriliest cat.
Branches reach out, each takes a dare,
One nearly lost its favorite pair!

The moon peeks out, a silver tease,
While acorns tumble with the breeze.
A chipmunk giggles, plays his trump,
As shadows gather, giving a jump.

The bark's all laugh lines, tells its tale,
Of storms and picnics, every detail.
A distant hoot, an echo's jest,
As nature responds, better than the rest.

So when the sun dips low and fades,
Join the trees in their merry charades.
In this twilight glow, humor flows,
Like laughter echoing where no one knows.

Songs of the Lithe Branches

The branches sway with funky tunes,
Dancing under the cheerful moons.
A funky bird, with shoes so bright,
Sang high notes, it took to flight!

Crickets chirp their rhythmic beat,
The leaves join in, oh what a feat!
They tap their toes on the soft ground,
In this dance-off, joy abounds.

A playful breeze, a cheeky tease,
Trips over roots, sets hearts at ease.
Twigs clapped hands, and laughter grew,
Under stars, the skies turned blue.

So raise your voices, join their throng,
For nature's spirit sings along.
In songs of mirth, we find our way,
In every night, a bright ballet.

Nature's Whispers in the Thicket

Squirrels chatter, plotting schemes,
Nuts fly high, just like my dreams.
A raccoon steals my sandwich wide,
While a robin cackles, full of pride.

The grasshoppers hop, jump for a prize,
Doing the tango right under the skies.
A crow calls out, 'You missed my joke!'
While I'm here pondering, time to provoke!

Trees sway gently, their trunks in a twist,
They tease the breeze as it gives them a lift.
Oh, woodland revelers parade around,
Under their branches, hilarity's found!

In the shade of green, laughter doth grow,
Nature's comedy show, 'Oh no!' and 'Whoa!'
With every rustle, a giggle takes flight,
Nature, you jest, but what a delight!

Harmonies Above the Leafy Cloak

High atop branches, a cuckoo sings,
Amusing the sparrows with his silly flings.
Down below, ants march in formation,
Lost in a world of strong concentration.

A bluejay squawks, trying to impress,
While a shy little finch just feels the stress.
They chirp and chime in awkward duets,
Making the woods feel like broadway bets.

A breeze tickles leaves, oh what a ruse!
They swish and sway, revealing their blues.
A big old oak shakes its mighty limbs,
Challenging the dancers to take some spins!

With laughter entwined, the branches do sway,
Nature's own band in a comical play.
Each note a chuckle, each pause a thrill,
To see the woods giggle gives me a chill!

Dreaming Under the Green Canopy

Mushrooms giggle beneath a tall tree,
'Can you believe how full I'm gonna be?'
The daisies roll, spreading their cheer,
Telling the sun, 'We're glad you're here!'

A snail comes sliding, all shiny and slow,
Says to a worm, 'Enjoy the show!'
While grass blades giggle, tickled by flight,
They sway in the sun, oh what a sight!

The clouds above share quiet confessions,
Filling the sky with all sorts of questions.
A playful platypus joins in the fun,
Whispering secrets of how to be one!

Wind whispers sweetly, stirring the dreams,
Nature's own laughter flows in streams.
In this joyful place, under skies so bright,
I'll keep on smiling in pure delight!

A Dance of Light and Air

Fireflies twinkle with a flashy wink,
'Can you catch us?' they laugh, 'Take a drink!'
A butterfly flutters in a giggly waltz,
'Who's chasing whom?' it ponders, then halts.

The shadows of leaves do pirouettes bold,
In a ballet of antics, they tease the old.
While an elder tree chuckles from its core,
'Back in my day, we danced on the floor!'

With each step, the brambles tap their toes,
And laughter erupts where the wildflower grows.
The sun beams down, its rays take a bow,
Turning this thicket into a crowd wow!

In the theater of nature, the humor is ripe,
Light twirls with air, with laughter in type.
So join in the dance, let joy take a flight,
In the green theater under the moonlight!

Leafy Lullabies and Echoed Dreams

In the trees a whisper plays,
Branches sway in silly ways,
Leaves applaud the wind's great show,
Dancing twigs with quite the glow.

Squirrels chatter, plotting fun,
Jumping high, they twist and run,
A leaf drops; it makes a sound,
Furry friends come leaping 'round.

Caterpillars start to groove,
Unbeknownst to their next move,
They munch on greens, so unaware,
Of all the giggles in the air.

Underneath the branches wide,
Nature's antics do abide,
With silly songs the moments gleam,
Creating laughter in the dream.

The Art of Stillness in the Trees

Beneath the oaks, a curious sight,
A chipmunk dons a hat so tight,
With acorns stacked like little cakes,
He poses hard; oh, the mistakes!

A rabbit hops right up to see,
And asks with glee, "Is that for me?"
They share a feast of leafy snacks,
And giggle at the oddball hacks.

The sun peeks in to join the fun,
A shadow puppet on the run,
Leaves throw shapes—an octopus!
Nature's laugh is quite a plus!

In quiet corners, secrets bloom,
As butterflies escape the gloom,
They flutter by with silly twirls,
In this still world where laughter swirls.

Nature's Breath in the Silver Shadows

In silver light, the shadows dance,
A raccoon stumbles, takes a chance,
With eyes as wide as dinner plates,
He spins about—oh, the silliness awaits!

Overhead the branches sway,
As if to join the wondrous play,
A little frog hops with such cheer,
Croaking jokes we all can hear.

A thundercloud with a funny face,
Watches closely this lively race,
As owls titter on a branch,
For every time, there's a chance to prance.

With whispered laughs the evening grows,
In nature's grip, the fun just flows,
With every sound, a story beams,
In shadow's play, we weave our dreams.

Time Stands Still Amidst the Saplings

The saplings giggle, stretching high,
Their leaves tickle the watchful sky,
A ladybug with polka dot flair,
Waves to the breeze; it's quite the affair!

Patched with moss, the ground lies soft,
Where critters bounce and frolic oft,
A turtle takes his time to peek,
Then hides again—he's so unique!

The sunbeams dance like little sprites,
While shadows play in silly flights,
A dogwood tree tells a joke,
And laughter rings; oh, it's no hoax!

In this moment, clock hands freeze,
As nature chuckles with such ease,
Time meanders, never in haste,
In sapling's arms, it's a merry place.

Whispers of the Refreshing Sky

The leaves are gossiping up high,
They tickle branches, oh so spry.
A squirrel nods, wearing a hat,
Chasing shadows, where's he at?

The clouds are chuckling, making jokes,
While pine trees join in with pokes.
A woodpecker's a stand-up star,
Telling tales from near and far.

A breeze slips through, giving a wink,
Tugging at branches, in sync.
The daisies dance, no shoes required,
While all around, the laughter's inspired.

As twilight casts a giggling shade,
The trees stand tall, their pranks displayed.
In the sky, the moon starts to beam,
Joining in this nighttime dream.

Tales of Trees and Wandering Winds

A poplar sways with silly glee,
While winds play tag, oh can't you see?
The oak is laughing, roots on display,
Saying, 'Come join! Let's play all day!'

The willows spill secrets, soft and sweet,
While cheeky raccoons dance on their feet.
A gust laughs loudly, causing a flare,
As pinecones tumble, unaware of the dare.

The fern is tickled by a nearby sprout,
Then starts to sneeze; oh, what a rout!
A butterfly giggles, trying to land,
On a cactus wearing shades, oh so grand!

As the sun sinks low, excitement grows,
The branches bow, the night bestows.
The forest's tales mix with the night,
In quirky laughter, all feels right.

Evocations of Verdant Eternity

In emerald halls where giggles roam,
The trees wear crowns, feeling at home.
With whispers soft, they share a jest,
While lizards lounge, all snug and blessed.

A playful breeze runs through the glade,
Around each trunk, a merry parade.
The frogs join in with croaks so loud,
As crickets chirp, it's quite a crowd!

Moss carpets ground like a fuzzy quilt,
With shadows dancing, oh what a guilt!
The ferns do a jig, 'til dawn's first light,
In this realm of green, pure delight.

With every rustle, a story unfolds,
Of past companions, brave and bold.
In verdant whispers, joy's spun pure,
An everlasting bond, hearts allure.

Hushed Conversations in the Clearings

In hidden spots where shadows play,
The trees exchange a quirk each day.
A laughing brook joins in with cheer,
   As squirrels plot, a sneaky leer.

Leafy crannies, all aglow,
Whisper secrets only they know.
The sunbeams giggle, tickling the rest,
   As the thicket shares its joyful zest.

Breezy puns float through the air,
While raccoons argue without a care.
Gravity's prank as apples fall,
   A comical mess, they can't recall.

As dusk approaches, tales grow bold,
   In cozy corners, stories told.
With laughter ringing through the trees,
   Life hums softly, swayed by the leaves.

Whirlwinds in the Wild

In the woods, a squirrel prances,
Windy gusts, it takes its chances.
With a twist and a turn, it slips,
Doing acrobatics, look at those flips!

A rabbit hops, trying to race,
But the wind tickles its little face.
"Hey, slow down!" it squeaks in delight,
While chasing its shadow, what a silly sight!

Leaves spin like dancers, twirling around,
Creating a ruckus without making a sound.
Nature's comedians put on a show,
Laughter erupts where the wild things go!

As the sun sets, the antics slow down,
But the forest still wears a playful crown.
In the mayhem, there's joy to be found,
Where the wind plays the fool, all around!

Silken Currents of Air

Whispers of laughter float on the breeze,
Tickling the leaves, with such gentle ease.
The butterflies giggle, their wings take flight,
As a curious snail plans a race for the night!

With a leap and a bound, a frog gives a cheer,
Its friends are all laughing, "We're right over here!"
They hop in a circle, then slip in a puddle,
"Who knew air could cause such a muddle?"

A few fuzzy bees, in a wobbly line,
Buzzing in rhythm, oh, what a design!
With each little dance, they trip over blooms,
Crafting a symphony of clumsy costumes.

As dusk falls around, the fun never ends,
Even the owls, they giggle, my friends!
In this world of fun, all creatures unite,
On silken currents, they dance through the night!

Ferns and Whispers: A Gentle Embrace

Underneath the ferns, the whispers arise,
"Did you hear that?" a bustling ant cries.
It's a breeze holding secrets so light,
While dandelion seeds take their flight!

A hedgehog rolls by in a jolly old trance,
Spreading the word—"Come join our dance!"
With each little wiggle, they shimmy and sway,
Nature's own party, hip-hip-hooray!

Breezy giggles rustle the grass,
As a worm wriggles by with plenty of sass.
"Hey, watch me wiggle, I'm the life of this show!"
But the beetles just chuckle, "You've got quite a glow!"

Amidst ferns and shadows, friendships do bloom,
In this funny cradle, there's all of the room.
With soft little nudges, the whispers embrace,
A humor-filled home, in this cozy place!

Murmuring Canopies at Dawn

Morning unveils, with giggles in flow,
The trees whisper tales of fun from below.
"Who did that?" chuckles the wise old oak,
While the breeze shares the gossip, the jokes it bespoke!

The sun peeks in, at the start of the show,
And the branches burst out with a hearty glow.
The woodpecker taps with rhythm so sly,
Clowning around, bidding good day to the sky!

A flock of birds starts a morning parade,
Flapping and flailing, oh what a charade!
With a jump and a flap, one falls with a thud,
And laughter erupts, despite the big thud!

As day starts to stretch, the fun won't retreat,
With murmurs of joy, the friends all repeat.
In this canopy world, where laughter takes flight,
Each dawn brings new tales of delight!

Sway of the Green Canopy

The branches wiggle in a silly dance,
A squirrel spins 'round, quite lost in chance.
The leaves shake hands, a leafy meet,
While birds drop down for a quick seat.

A gust pulls hats from folks below,
As laughter floats where warm winds blow.
Each twig a comedian in disguise,
With chuckles hiding under the skies.

The trunks are groaning with delight,
As shadows whirl in playful light.
Together they twirl, in spunky cheer,
Nature's giggles, loud and clear!

So let your worries drift away,
Join the fun where the green leaves play.
In this frolicsome show we see,
The goofiest side of a grand old tree.

Whirl of Leaves and Light

The leaves are whirlwinds of playful grace,
Doing cartwheels in a leafy race.
Sunshine winks between their flares,
As if it's tickling with golden stares.

A gentle puff turns a hat askew,
Causing laughter among the crew.
The shadows leap, a merry sight,
Turning even the dullest day bright.

Round and round, the acorns roll,
As critters jive in nature's stroll.
Each rustle and giggle, a soft serenade,
Creating a scene where the players parade.

So take a hint from the swirling light,
Join the frolic, chase away fright.
With every swell, let joy ignite,
In the merry whirl of the day so bright.

The Dance of Nature's Breath

Oh, how the branches sashay and sway,
In a gusty song, they come out to play.
The grass is jittery, a green ballet,
As twigs shimmied in the sun's soft ray.

The flowers giggle like kids in a park,
As butterflies flutter, making their mark.
The air is tickled with whispers and laughs,
As nature performs in her own arts and crafts.

A jestful breeze messes up the line,
As critters gossip about the sunshine.
With every tug, they break into rhyme,
In this lighthearted jest of nature's prime.

So let your spirit join this spree,
And sway to the whims of the leaf and tree.
In this grand dance, find your own part,
And share a giggle straight from the heart.

Soft Light Between the Bark

Whispers of laughter between the trees,
Where shadows play and sway with ease.
The sunlight peeks through a leafy crack,
Casting silly shapes in colors that pop back.

A chatty chipmunk climbs with a grin,
As sunlight dances on his furry skin.
The trunks lean in, sharing a joke,
While nearby flowers giggle and croak.

A rustling gust gives everyone glee,
As hats take flight nearby an old bee.
The world is tickled by nature's fun,
While branches clap, saying, "We've just begun!"

So take a moment, watch and see,
The joy that blooms in the shade of a tree.
In the playful light that flits and sparks,
Find laughter lurking soft, between the bark.

Echoes of the Summer Air

The sunbeams dance with lazy flair,
A squirrel scrambles without a care.
He stumbles, twirls in leafy plight,
Who knew acorns could be so light?

Jackets hang on branches like lost dreams,
Chasing ribbons caught in playful schemes.
Bees gossip loudly, buzzing about,
While ants march past, avoiding a drought.

Treetop Serenade at Dusk

A woodpecker's rhythm clicks with zest,
The raccoons laugh; they know the best.
They take a bow on a branch so low,
While shadows play hide and seek in a row.

Crickets try their hand at a lullaby,
Missed the note; they just sigh and try.
The fireflies blink, competing for stars,
While owls give wise winks from afar.

Sunlit Shadows and Hushed Hums

A fluffy cloud drifts like a tease,
While the sun laughs at busy bees.
They fumble in flowers, their fashion fades,
Getting stuck in petals, creating charades.

Dandelion wishes float like a joke,
As children giggle, they turn up the smoke.
The grass offers each tiny toe a tickle,
A rustling burst, oh, what a pickle!

Memories Carried on the Wind

The gusts carry tales from yesterday,
Of dogs in hats that loved to play.
They'd prance and dance, what a silly sight,
Causing kites to lift with all their might.

Leaves chatter softly, exchanging old lines,
About the boy who made up rhymes.
He tripped, he laughed, and fell with flair,
Who knew that grass had such a snare?

Nature's Caress in the Glade

In a forest of winks, the trees like to sway,
Whispers of laughter in this leafy ballet.
Squirrels wear goggles, they leap and they twirl,
Nature's a jester, giving us a whirl.

Chirping of crickets, a comedic show,
Dance-floor of shadows, with barely a toe.
The flowers start giggling, a colorful jest,
While ants do the shuffle, they're simply the best.

Sunbeams are chuckling, they tickle the ground,
Pinecones are rolling, they make a soft sound.
With nature's own humor, it's all quite absurd,
A symphony played by the laugh of a bird.

So let's raise a toast to this playful parade,
Where even the fungi have jokes to invade.
In every small rustle, the fun takes a stroll,
Nature's wild laughter is good for the soul!

A Dance of Petals and Wind

Petals are prancing, they swirl like a clown,
Tickled by gusts, they tumble down.
Bees buzz with laughter, they hum a nice tune,
While daisies play tag 'neath the big, friendly moon.

Wind pulls the threads of a flirty grass dress,
Tree trunks are giggling, they simply confess.
Each leaf has a story, a quirky little spin,
They whisper in chorus, let the fun times begin!

The brook runs with chuckles, it splashes with cheer,
Even the stones laugh, if you know how to hear.
Clouds puff up softly, they're teasing the sun,
In this garden of joy, there's always more fun.

So spin with the petals, embrace the delight,
Nature's a comedian, all day and all night.
Let laughter be carried on swift summer winds,
In the dance of the flowers, where whimsy begins!

Tranquil Tunes of the Treetops

The treetops are crooning a laid-back cheer,
With whispers of giggles that float through the sphere.
Branches sway to rhythms, a leafy serenade,
Birds in a chorus, their jokes never fade.

The owls wear spectacles, they're wise but quite sly,
While foxes play chess 'neath the watchful sky.
Hoots and the howls meld in a whimsical blend,
As laughter flows freely, it never will end.

The rustle of leaves is a chuckling tune,
Under the sun and the bright honey moon.
Bees twirl and dip, like they're out on a spree,
Nature's ensemble is funny and free.

So sit for a moment, just soak in the sound,
In this room of the trees, where joy knows no bound.
Their tranquil tunes tease a soft, silly side,
In the haven of whispers, let laughter abide!

The Poetry of Quiet Stirrings

In the hush of the night, the shadows conspire,
To tickle the light with their whimsy and fire.
Mice make a muffle, their jokes quite absurd,
As the moon starts to giggle, not caring who heard.

Whispers in grass become playful and bright,
Crickets tell tales that can last till the light.
The stars up above are all winking, it seems,
While nightingales chuckle and weave silly dreams.

A rustle of feathers, the owls wink and show,
That night time's a stage with a wild, funny glow.
In this quiet of stirrings, where joy takes its flight,
Every shadow will dance, coaxed by laughter's delight.

So let's celebrate moments of soft, silly grace,
In the poetry written on nature's warm face.
For in every small stirring, there's humor to find,
In the playground of night, we're all intertwined!

Interlude of Green and Blue

In a dance of green, the branches sway,
Leaves giggle softly in a playful display.
Squirrels debate on the best climbing flair,
While rabbits take bets on a game of air.

A skunk in the shade gives a wink of delight,
As fireflies flash, twinkling into the night.
Chirping birds gossip on who's the best flier,
A leaf drops down, calling out, "You're a liar!"

With whispers of laughter, the nature unfolds,
Where each little critter has stories untold.
In shadows of wonder, the tales seem to bloom,
As the sun drips honey, sweetening the gloom.

The trees wear their crowns made of laughter and light,
While underfoot critters prepare for a flight.
In this quirky show, all are welcome to cheer,
For the whims of the forest bring hijinks sincere.

Mysteries in the Treetops

In the tangled branches, a detective bird,
Hiccups and flutters, much too absurd.
"Who stole my acorn?" he squawks with a grin,
A squirrel jumps down, singing, "Let's begin!"

Ladybugs gossip, "Did you see that? Wow!"
A raccoon rolls by, acting like a cow.
Laughter cascades through the forest so wide,
As mysteries tumble and secrets collide.

The shadowed limbs hold stories quite grand,
A frog croaks a clue: "It was squirrel, not band!"
The trees hold their breath as each clue chimes a tune,
While mushy old mushrooms hum under the moon.

With each twist and turn, the silliness grown,
In the court of the woods, wisdom is shown.
The great thief of acorns is finally known,
And friendships grow deep in this laughter-filled cone.

The Essence of Wood and Air

Woodpeckers drum on the trees with a beat,
Singing their anthems to the critters in fleet.
Breezes blow softly, a tickling affair,
While ants march in lines, determined, yet fair.

A beehive buzzes, sharing jokes on the go,
While butterflies flutter, "To the dance floor, let's flow!"
The willow bows low, as if telling a jest,
"Join the fun, little ones, in this feathered nest!"

The sun peeks through, a spotlight so bright,
As shadows play tag, avoiding the light.
In the playful expanse of this woodland ballet,
Every creature joins in, without dismay.

Leaves clap their hands in this joyous parade,
Wood and air mingle in a whimsical jade.
Each heart shares a chuckle, a bond we all share,
In this forest, the essence of life's in the air!

Time's Gentle Touch on the Leaves

As the clock tick-tocks, the leaves take a spin,
A waltz in the sunlight, where silliness begins.
Trees chuckle softly, sharing their tales,
Of soft summer whispers and autumn's pink veils.

Each moment's a snapshot, a giggle on wind,
As critters all gather, their laughter rescinds.
A turtle insists he's the fastest around,
Yet slow as molasses, he's stuck to the ground.

The sun plays peek-a-boo with shadows and beams,
While owls roll their eyes, sipping sweet dreams.
The breeze gently nudges the branches just so,
As time gently dances, a delightful show.

In this pocket of wonder where time wears a hat,
Squirrels prank each other, and giggles are fat.
For every leaf falling tells secrets to keep,
Where the whispers of nature invite us to leap.

Echoes of Youth in the Verdant Shade

In the park, we twist and spin,
Chasing each other, grins so wide.
Squirrels watch, they plot, begin,
To steal our snacks, oh, what a ride!

Sunshine winks through leafy hats,
We roll on grass, so green, so bright.
But watch your head, oh, silly cats,
That tree branch swings, it's quite a fright!

Giggles ring as we climb high,
Daredevils soar on ropes so bold.
We reach for clouds, touch the sky,
Don't tell the grown-ups, we've been told!

Then we tumble in a heap,
Laughter flows like a bubbling brook.
Memory's treasure we will keep,
Let's sneak a peek at storybooks!

Tangles of Light and Air's Embrace

Caught in a swirl of sunlit glee,
We dance like leaves, oh, what a sight!
A twist, a turn, so wild and free,
Our shadows grow long, but spirits bright.

A kite goes up, it dips and dives,
While we chase it down with squeals of joy.
A tree stump's throne where laughter thrives,
We crown ourselves, no rules to annoy!

With cookie crumbs on our small hands,
We giggle at ants with work so grand.
Off we scamper to far-off lands,
In our wild games, we take a stand!

Who knows what tomorrow may bring?
For now, we're kings and queens of play.
Under the shade, we laugh and sing,
In our secret world, come dance and sway!

Whispers Through the Leaves

Listen close, the trees confide,
Secrets of giggles hid in their bark.
The rustling leaves, a friend by our side,
They tickle our ears when it gets dark.

A sneaky breeze, it loves to tease,
It steals our hats with a playful whiff.
We chase it down, oh, what a spree,
What's next, a tree-climbing cliff?

Bark on our knees from our silly falls,
We invent a game of leap and shout.
With echoing laughter through leafy halls,
We're tiny warriors, there's no doubt!

At dusk we rest, worn out but bright,
Telling tales of our glorious day.
In nature's arms, everything feels right,
We'll share these whispers, come what may!

Dancing Shadows in the Canopy

Under the shade, we spin and twirl,
Like mischievous sprites, we run amok.
A flip, a skip, we tumble and whirl,
Our laughter echoes, oh, what a shock!

Caught on a branch, a shoe lost,
The squirrels giggle as if in jest.
Oh, what a price for our fun-filled cost,
With no shoes left, we're still the best!

Pine cones become our mighty swords,
In battles fought, we'll never lose.
With make-believe dragons in our hoards,
In this vibrant world, we gladly choose!

As shadows stretch, we plan our route,
Adventure calls, we can't be still.
So off we go, with joyous shout,
To conquer our kingdom, the world to thrill!

Enveloping Warmth in Nature's Embrace

In the sway of trees, a giggle stirs,
Leaves rustle as if sharing blurs.
A squirrel in shades, a hat askew,
Dances to rhythms of sky so blue.

The sunlight chuckles, casting a glow,
Tickling the grass where the wildflowers grow.
A butterfly trips on its flight plan,
Wings flapping wildly, oh what a scam!

A bumblebee buzzes, all full of glee,
Trying to chat up a daisy's spree.
Yet the daisy just yawns, it ought to know,
That love blooms best when you take it slow!

The breeze plays tag, a cheeky sprite,
Whirling through branches, a playful sight.
Nature's laughter, oh what a sound,
In this hug of warmth, joy's always found!

Softly Spoken Secrets of the Soul

Whispers of leaves, secrets galore,
A chipmunk relays tales of yore.
The air's full of giggles, a raucous tune,
As clouds poke fun at a sunlit moon.

The brook babbles softly, sharing a jest,
While sunbeams tease, for they never rest.
A rabbit lifts ears, listening keen,
To the drumming of frogs, in between.

A wise old owl hoots a comic line,
Says the stars are all buddies, how sweetly they shine!
And the fireflies dance, lighting the scene,
In this quiet theater, life's a routine.

Together they chuckle, a whimsical crew,
Nature's delight, a hilariously true.
In playful banter, they frolic and roll,
Softly spoken secrets, the heart and the soul!

The Gentle Embrace of Nature's Hand

In the crook of a branch, a tiny bird swings,
Singing a ditty about silly things.
The flowers reply, in colors that flash,
As giggles erupt with each joyful splash.

The brook takes a leap, splashing in jest,
While a turtle watches, truly impressed.
A wind-blown hat takes a run through the trees,
As blossoms all chuckle, carried with ease.

Clouds in a cluster, playing hide and seek,
Making shadows that dance, so bold yet meek.
A grasshopper hops, with the greatest of flair,
Telling tall tales without a care.

Oh, nature's embrace, so tender and spry,
With laughter that echoes under the sky.
In this gentle hold, we find our delight,
A funny little world, all merry and bright!

The Mischief of a Whispering Wind

The wind kicks up trouble with a playful huff,
Tickling the trees, can't seem to get enough.
It steals a hat and runs with a grin,
Watch out! Here it comes, let the chaos begin!

The daisies nod, trying hard not to giggle,
As the gust plays tricks, it gives them a wiggle.
A funny parade of leaves takes flight,
Whirling and twirling in pure delight.

It whispers sweet nothings to birds up high,
Painting the blue with a dreamy sigh.
Yet back to the ground, it swoops with a tease,
Bumping a rabbit who stumbles with ease!

Oh, the mischief it brings, the trouble it makes,
Laughing through valleys and skipping through lakes.
In its playful dance, it crafts such a sight,
The whispering wind, a jester in flight!

www.ingramcontent.com/pod-product-compliance
Lightning Source LLC
Chambersburg PA
CBHW072146200426
43209CB00051B/755